Differently Daphne

Written by **Adrianne Free** *Illustrated by* **Marussia**

Published by Parker & Co., LLC
P.O. Box 50040
Richmond, VA 23250

ISBN (paperback): 978-1-952733-28-4
ISBN (hardback): 978-1-952733-29-1
ISBN (ebook): 978-1-952733-30-7

DEDICATION

To my goddaughter Savannah,
Your joy and love for reading warm my heart. During those priceless moments of sharing in your bedtime stories, I discovered how valuable storybooks like these are for young, developing, curious minds. You were my motivation. Thank you.

To my parents,
Thank you for always providing me the freedom and encouragement to believe beyond my limitations. Because of you, I approach life with the anticipation of what I can do instead of what I can't, and that has taken me far. I am forever grateful. I love you.

THIS BOOK
BELONGS TO:

_____

Dear Young Readers,

One exciting day in February, my mom was super ready to meet me. Her sweet precious baby girl had been making a home in her stomach for many months. She had seen me before, but only in a picture on a little TV screen. I had the perfect little hands, legs, arms, and feet. Everything was normal.

But when I was born, something went wrong. The only way the doctors could save my life resulted in a serious injury to the nerves in my left shoulder. My arm didn't move much. It just hung by my side. My mom became really sad and concerned. The doctor told her that my injury was called Erb's Palsy and that my new little life would require multiple surgeries and years of physical therapy. He was right, but he left a few things out. First, my arm would look a little different. Second, I would not be able to do the same things in the same way as my friends. And third, some days I would get sad or frustrated about it. All those things became true.

But through my parents' encouragement and their hope for me not to be held back by my disability, I learned I was able to do everything that everyone else could do, just *differently*. If you ask my mom, she'll tell you that it all started when I was learning to tie my shoes. I was determined! When she tried to help, I pushed her hand away. That worked most of the time, unless we were running late. She knew she had to allow me to learn to do things on my own so that I wouldn't always have to depend on someone else. Even if I got frustrated, she had to make the hard decision of when to help and when not to help.

You see, it all worked out in the end because everything I mastered boosted my confidence, and nothing could stop me from being in dance recitals, roller-skating, playing basketball, playing musical instruments, and anything else I desired to do because I believed I could. My hope is that you, too, will find the confidence to live beyond your limitations, embrace your differences, and never give up!

Your cheerleader,

Adrianne Free

P.S. You will have the opportunity to affirm your own confidence and strength by writing your own name in the blank on page 23. Make your name beautiful, colorful, and bold!

Differently Daphne was ready to play
with two new friends she met that day.
They laughed and giggled and twirled in their shoes,
excited to learn what they were going to do.

"Look, Daphne! Look! It's a new relay game with monkey bars, tunnels, and fun squishy things."

"Wait! Wait! We cannot start! My shoestrings are not tied."
"Do you not know how to do it? We tied our shoes inside."
"I don't know how. My arm won't work. I wish I was like you."
"Don't be sad. It's okay. One day you will learn, too."

"Ms. Piper, we need help. Can you help her tie her shoe?"
"Sure, I will! It's okay. Sometimes I need help, too."
"Ok, Daphne, you're ready to go. Put a smile on that sweet face.
Everyone's so excited to start the silly relay race."

"Remember, children, you will start when I say go,
and if you want to win, your team cannot be slow.
Each team must do it all. You cannot pick and choose.
And if you don't complete it, sadly your team will lose."

"Ready, Set, Go!" Ms. Piper yelled, and the first person started the race.Maddie was first for my team. She ran fast to set the pace.Up the stairs, through the bridge, and down the slide she went. Over the bars, around the cone, and through the little tent.

"Go, Maddie! Go, Maddie! Only one more thing to do.
Get the balloons to the other side, and you must carry two."

"Tiptoe fast or slow, hold them high, or hold them low. Swish, swish, flippity flop! Don't let your balloons go ploppity plop!"

Hooray! Hooray! She made it through. Now it's time for person two. Chloe ran as fast as she could and finished the first part just as good.

Time for the balloons, the hardest part,
and though she went slow, she passed the mark.
Wow, they're good! My friends are great!
I always knew I had the best teammates.

This is it. It's up to me. I'm last to go. I'm person three.
Through the bridge and down the slide,
the other team is close behind.
Around the cone, through the tent—wait, but wait! I can't do this.

I can only carry one.
My other hand won't work.
I tried to carry it anyway,
but now it's in the dirt.

"We won! We won!" the other team cheered.
They were all so happy and glad.

But my team lost because of me,
and it made me really sad.

"It's okay, Daphne! Wipe your eyes.
You did your very best.
Yeah, Daphne, we're not mad.
It's not like it's a test.
Ms. Piper, will we play again?"
"Yes, very, very soon."
"Now we'll have another chance to
show them that girls rule."

I don't know. I'm just sad. My hand will never change.
So even if we play again, it will all be just the same.
"Let's go, girls. It's time to go. Your buses are now here."
"No matter what, we're friends forever. We will always be right here."

"Hi, my sweet Daphne, how was your day?
Did you learn something cool, or did you play all day?"
"Yeah, but no, I guess so. I don't really care.
My friends can do everything, but I can't do anything. It's just not fair."

"Everything was fine until we played the game."
"Ok, tell me what happened; tell me what changed."

"Well, we were winning and we were going fast,
and then it was my turn, and we finished last."

"It's all my fault, I could not do it right.
I dropped the balloon because I can't hold it tight.
My arm is the problem, and it will never change.
Will I always have Erb's Palsy? Will it ever go away?"

"I know, baby, I know you're sad
and maybe frustrated, too,
but I want you to know your arm is not bad.
It just makes you uniquely you!
Some things will be easy and some things will be hard.
But you must not give up on yourself; believe with all your heart."

"When things become a challenge, you may have to sit and think,
'How can I get this done and do it *differently?*'
It may not be how your friends do it, but that's ok, you see.
Everyone can do the same, yet do it *differently!*"

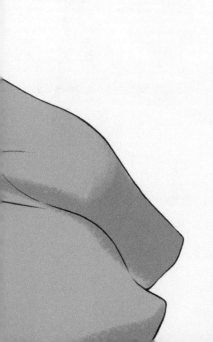

"It may help you to say these words when things challenge you a bit so you can be your own superhero and have more confidence."

"My name is , _____
and I believe in me.
I am strong and smart enough
to do this *differently!*"

"Mommy, Mommy, I like that! It already makes me feel strong!
Do you think it works at school or does it work only at home?"
"If you believe, it never leaves, and it will follow where you go.
And if you play the game tomorrow, try and see, and let me know."

"Ok, class, are you ready to play?
I think we'll play the game from yesterday!"
"Oh, yay! Perfect for me.
How did she know?
How could this be?!"

"Ready, Set, Go!" Ms. Piper yelled, and
Maddie was fast again.
Then Chloe was even faster, and now
I knew that we could win.

"Go, Daphne, Go!" my friends yelled and I knew it was up to me.
And when I saw the balloons, I thought to do it *differently.*

Oh, I know! I grabbed my shirt and held it with my hand.
I put the balloon inside and held the other one again.
Off I went, across the line, before the other team!
Yippie! We won and we did great, and I'm so proud of me!

ADRIANNE FREE

As a Certified Group Fitness Instructor and Dance Ministry Lead, Adrianne literally and figuratively dances to the beat of her own drum. She has a passion for encouraging and leading the next generation, first as a therapeutic recreational dance instructor for disabled teens and young adults and now weekly with the youth at her church. Though Adrianne has always had to navigate life *differently* with Erb's Palsy, she enjoys challenging herself to reach beyond her limits whether vacationing internationally, dancing on skates, or competing in speed typing contests--with one hand! This godmother of six, born in North Carolina, graduated from North Carolina A&T State University and now resides in Virginia.

CPSIA information can be obtained
at www.ICGtesting.com
Printed in the USA
BVHW021657230621
610223BV00013B/617

9 781952 733284